Her Eyes Tell a Story

Poetry of Love

Ivy Rose Elizalde

Instagram: ivroselizalde
Facebook Page: Ivy Rose
Twitter: ivros elizalde

Copyright © 2020
By Ivy Rose Elizalde
All Rights Reserved.
No part of this book may be reproduced or used in any manner without the express written permission of the author except the use of brief quotations in a book review.

For more information, email: eivyrose@yahoo.com

Acknowledgements

I want to thank God most of all for giving me the opportunity to write a book again. I almost forgot that writing a poetry was my first love since I was 13 years old. My first book "The Addiction to Success" is a far more different book genre, so I'm excited to share my second book which is a poetry about love.

I want to thank my family for being my inspiration for all my writings, my Papa Oscar, Mama Linda, Dennis, April, and Jimme.

They say that a person can effectively write if he can actually feel a certain kind of emotion. I believe we don't experience love and heartaches for no reasons. Everything serves a purpose in our lives. As for me, they are beautiful learnings that I would still thank those people who became a part of me for molding me for who I am now.

To all my friends who supports me in my writing and for believing in me, thank you.

Lastly, I would like to thank the person who's been there for me and accepts me for who I am. He also inspires and motivates me to write this book. And the one who gave me the emotions I needed to be able to fill the happy part of this book.

Contents

Introduction..1

Torn..3

Wisdom...71

Found...151

About the author...209

Introduction

This book is composed of short poems about love. An intense feeling of affection while struggling with pain. It also includes heartbreaks, separation, learnings, and eventually finding new hope to love again.

This is a poetry of mixed emotions that most of us are experiencing in life. A learning from these emotions gives us wisdoms, accepting pain as a tool to gain strength and to live with hope and purpose.

This book is for everyone who's experiencing the ups and down of love, whether in a relationship or not, this book will somewhat make you feel every emotions you have to come across in love.

It's a poetry way designed to make the words even stronger to feel and bare one's soul, making imaginations travel from a place of agonizing pain to immeasurable happiness.

It is a poetic journey of love that gives us an understanding of our life's purpose. Makes us realize more about love, about ourselves, and reflecting on how we handle our relationships. It also shows a lot of self-love and self-worth.

It is divided into 3 parts: torn, wisdom, and found.

"My heart was torn with your love."

Torn

Shallow

I realize that it's scarier
To fall deeply in love
So I let go while it's shallow.

Ivy Rose Elizalde

Broken Destiny

We were so in love
Like our souls were in-sync together
But as quick as a blink of an eye
Everything has shattered
We thought of it as an abrupt shift
Which was really a bizarre
Until we hear the word "broken destiny"
Finally it answers all our why's.

The First to Let Go

You may think it's a payback
For all the hurt that you've caused me
But you wouldn't understand
The agony to be the first to let go

Ivy Rose Elizalde

20-Second Shock

I was literally in 20-second shock
The moment you told me
You found someone else.

Blindsided

I was blindsided
You never made me feel
Your feelings have changed

Ivy Rose Elizalde

Movie

I can't help but cry as I see a funny movie
For this time I got no choice
But to laugh at it without you

Her Eyes Tell a Story

Haunted

The rain has stopped but left drizzles on air
I look for the sun but I see shadows
How can we be haunted by memories
Aren't they supposed to go
Where the wind vanishes its course

Ivy Rose Elizalde

Great Lesson

We tend to teach a great lesson to someone
In a way of letting them go.

No Traces

Our love left no traces
No one could ever say
That once in our life
We fell in love.

Ivy Rose Elizalde

The Last Person

You're the last person I thought
Who would have left me
Too much confidence
Couldn't be mistaken for trust

Tough Love

Does harsh word considered
A new expression of love?
Does breaking someone's heart
Become a license to passion?
It may be intense and all-consuming
But I don't want your tough love

Ivy Rose Elizalde

Candle

My love for you is like a candle
It outwears once used.

Draw

I wish to draw your face
To memorize your eyes
And be familiar with your cheeks
Learn the curves of your lips
So maybe goodbyes would be easy
If I have them in my memory

Ivy Rose Elizalde

Not The Perfect Two

I guess this love wasn't made to last
It isn't about the stars
And destiny shouldn't be blamed either
It's just that we're not the perfect two
Who knows how to give a fight

Dreams

How come it's just a dream
When I held you in my arms
It felt so real

Ivy Rose Elizalde

The Art of Walking Away

Silence can be loud
When all you can hear are heartbeats
And no one attempts to say a word
Because we know exactly
How to make it easier
It's the art of walking away

Her Eyes Tell a Story

The Day You Almost Died

If it hurts so much today
Believe me time will come
When you'll no longer remember
That day you almost died

Ivy Rose Elizalde

The Only Way

Sometimes the only way
To change a person for the better
Is to walk away

Misery

Never look back on situations
That once brought you misery
It's a pattern that you cannot change
It's either you live with it
Or you leave it.

Ivy Rose Elizalde

Don't Need Pain

They say you'll never know you're in love
If you don't feel the pain
But I don't need pain to realize
My understanding of love
Love connects everything
But not everything connects in love

Passerby

Everything was perfect until we realize
We're just passersby into each other's lives.

Ivy Rose Elizalde

Scared

She's scared if the time comes
When everything's so perfect
Eventually change in a second
Will you blame her?
She had seen so much in her past.

The Way to Love Me

Love me in a way
You do more than you say
Because I don't believe in promises
People are weak not to break them.

Ivy Rose Elizalde

This Will End Soon

I'm afraid I'm beginning to lose this love
The love I've been holding on for quite some time
It won't work no matter how hard I try
So I stand still and wait till the feelings die

Forgotten Memory

I've waited for this day
That when I think of you
I won't feel the love anymore
I was sure this day will come
That every pain you've caused me
Will become a forgotten memory

Ivy Rose Elizalde

Dare Me

If you think my heart is easy
For it beats just for you
Let me remind you
That this heart has same rhythm
Just before I met you
So dare me
'Cause I'm not afraid to break my heart.

I'm Not Okay

We thought love is enough to make this work
But even a strong love gets tired and subsides
So if one day you wonder what happened
Perhaps I figured out I'm not okay
But still I want you to know
That there are hundreds of times I fought to stay

Ivy Rose Elizalde

Fall to Fool

How could you make me fall?
Just to make me fool.

Resilent

Back to the silence of the ocean
No hassles and complications
Just like the two of us
Back to the silence of strangers

Ivy Rose Elizalde

Awaken

We were walking hand in hand
A strong feeling of attachment
That was close to a perfect love
Then we woke up in a reality
That you and I were just a dream

Favorite Pain

I once had a quiet life
Till you came and complicate everything
How can I get you off my mind
When you're my favorite pain.

Ivy Rose Elizalde

Spy

I caught you staring at me
How could you have such mysterious eyes
Like a spy who watches my every move
Trying to see if your bait is good
Don't try to fool me
I know the tricks you're playing
Don't spy with an identity

Broken Promise

Forgive me
If I can't hold on
To my promise
That you'll be
The last person I'll love.

Ivy Rose Elizalde

Felt Loved

Why does it feel like
The moment we let go
Is also the moment we felt loved?

Your Eyes

How could I not believe in you
When your eyes
Speak a melody I knew by heart
And I blame this heart
For not always being precise.

Ivy Rose Elizalde

Better

It is better to hurt myself
By letting you go
Than to bury my heart
In this kind of love

Hurt Enough

She's a woman
Who's been hurt enough
To waste another single tear
In a man
Who's not worth crying for

Ivy Rose Elizalde

Never Come Back

If there comes a time
You've got a change of heart
And fallen in love with someone else
Just tell me honestly
Because I'm willing to let you go
But please swear to me
That you'll never come back again

Cheater

I always forgive people
Who hurt me along the way
But since you're never sorry
I won't forget you anyway
Because I never forget a cheater

Ivy Rose Elizalde

I Can't Fall in Love

I can be the craziest woman in love
But I can't fall in love with someone
Whose heart will never be mine.

Fool

You think you can fool me
When I can see clearly and I'm not blind
I just fell in love with you
And you're a fool if you can't see it too

Ivy Rose Elizalde

Trace of the Past

I don't want to admit
That pain and betrayal from the past
Made my heart terrified
To fully love and trust again.

Let Me Go

My time is valuable to me
So if you're not sure about me
Please let me know
And let me go.

Ivy Rose Elizalde

Not Sorry

Don't say sorry
If you have an intention
Of doing it again.

Disgusting Change

You know what's the most disgusting change
It's when the person who treated you so special
Start out making you feel ordinary now

Ivy Rose Elizalde

Tired

My heart whispered "I'm tired"
So I let her rest for a while.

Lost Again

You gave your light to me
But then you took it away
Now I'm lost again

Ivy Rose Elizalde

Tattoo of Your Name

I want a tattoo of your name
Marked in my skin
The excruciating pain
The needle brings
Reminds me of our love
That's troubled with pain.

Rain

The rain feels like an old friend
Who never lets you cry alone.

Ivy Rose Elizalde

Rendezvous

Rendezvous can be a bittersweet
Memory of the past

I Thought

I thought we fell in love
Until I realized you just let me fall
Without the intention of loving me at all.

Ivy Rose Elizalde

Good Morning Text

The first thing I have to get used to
Is to look at my phone
Without checking
For a good morning text from you.

Silent Goodbye

I know someday
You would thank me
For my silent goodbye

Ivy Rose Elizalde

Knife

Can you just kill me with a knife?
Because your words are more painful
Than the actual pain of death.

December Feels

The hurt you've caused just fade away
At times I doubt if you've ever existed
But the strange thing I never forget
Is how sad it feels during December.

Ivy Rose Elizalde

Deep Exhaustion

When two people
Haven't fallen out of love
But decided to part ways
Perhaps one of them
Has got tired of fighting alone
Deep exhaustion of soul and mind
Is a savage emotion

Stayed

I never dreamt of that kind of love
A torture in my heart
A wound in my soul
But then I thought
That love was for me to keep
So I stayed.

Ivy Rose Elizalde

Almost

Our story was like a movie
With a twist and mystery
But it ends with an almost
"We almost fell in love."

Wind Passing By

I once dreamt of your love
Like I thought it would be a perfect picture
Of a love I've always prayed for
But you're like a wind passing by
With no intention of loving me
So I walk away.

Ivy Rose Elizalde

Liar

If I see you again
I won't look at your eyes
Not because I'm afraid to fall again
But because those eyes remind me
How good they can lie.

Her Eyes Tell a Story

Beautiful Soul

You said she's a beautiful soul
But you hurt her even so.

Ivy Rose Elizalde

Survive

Ocean reminds me of big waves
That flooded me
I was drowning and shouting for help
But no one came
I wanted to surrender
But then I told myself, "Not today."
I won't die on this water
I have to figure out how to survive
To witness the greatness of life
And the real purpose
Of a broken heart.

Terrible Hurt

I forgot how you said it
The things I once wish
To disappear on my mind
But now I can't recall
Even your face I once wish
To stare for the rest of my life
Except that I never forget
How you made me feel
'Cause it's terrible hurt.

Ivy Rose Elizalde

Jealousy

Jealousy is just a form of self-doubt
Often instilled to us by the person we love
If they could just give us peace of mind
Perhaps we could feel that we're more than enough.

Wall

You put a wall on us
So I can't hurt you
But that wall
Destroyed us.

Ivy Rose Elizalde

I Don't Need Your Love

Don't tell me the things
I wish you would have told me before
Because I don't need your love anymore

"Only a person who can love genuinely has the courage to find wisdom in love."

Wisdom

Wisdom of Love

My hand can't stop writing about love
I realized I have so many emotions
Compiled through these years
To be able to write a poetry
Because the truth is love can make us happy
But pain can make us wise

Ivy Rose Elizalde

Arts of Love

I must have to travel the world
To see the real beauty of love
Because I've learned
That pain and happiness
Are the two different arts of love

Butterflies

I look at you and find out
Why butterflies tend to go inside our stomach
It's not to celebrate a love that's rare
But to give us a feeling
Of joy of being imprisoned

Ivy Rose Elizalde

First Love

First love is sweet but innocent
We thought life is merely about falling in love
Not knowing that happy ever after exists
Possibly not just in fairy tales
But rarely in our first love

No Excuse

Don't take heartaches as an excuse
To lose faith in love
Because love will never be wrong
Only the people we chose to love
Could be the wrong ones.

Ivy Rose Elizalde

Unconditional Love

Unconditional love is the most mysterious thing in this world
That even the most intelligent people can't rationalize.

The Wisdom of a Broken Glass

A cup of glass may fall into pieces
And never return to its purpose
But it's more than just a piece of the cup now
Just like the heart that once broken
It may never be the same again
But the pieces it become tends to offer more
A piece of love to give, a piece of strength
A piece of happiness, a piece of calm, a piece self-love
A piece of faith, a piece of contentment
A piece of understanding, a piece of fair and honesty
A piece of loving life
No book or people in this earth could teach you
The wisdom only the pain of a broken heart could tell

Ivy Rose Elizalde

The Wonders of a Broken Heart

Every person must experience to be heartbroken even once in their lives
A life would never be great without that part of the story

Reflection

You smile and he smiles back
He does to you what you do for him
That's how people works
So when love isn't reciprocated
Give a little more
Trust me one day
When that person you love the most
Becomes your reflection

Ivy Rose Elizalde

Gamer's Love

I want someone who will look at me
Like I'm his favorite game
'Cause I know he'll be focused
And no distraction can drag him
But if you'll ask me
Why would I settle for a game
It's because I knew
That for him it's a serious thing

Ironic

Some people let us go because they think
They are not good enough for us
But we hold on because we think
No one could ever love them as we do

Ivy Rose Elizalde

Mistakes

It's okay to commit mistakes in love
Make a lot of mistakes
But don't waste your time
Making the same mistakes
With the same dumb person
You still have in your life right now
Preferably make new mistakes

Ruin

It's easy to forget a person
Who has been a jerk and mean to you
But the one who once gave you his world
Could ruin your soul forever

Ivy Rose Elizalde

Memories

Sometimes we don't actually miss the person
We just miss their memories.

Blue Rose

Have you ever found a real blue rose?
'Cause I never found one
But like true love I know they exist.

Ivy Rose Elizalde

Don't Turn Your Back

Don't turn your back to someone
'Cause when you do
You will have to travel the world
To find that person again
Who will truly love you.

Time

They said love
Is the most important thing in this world
But they are wrong
It's the time, perfect time.

Ivy Rose Elizalde

Worthy

Sometimes we give too many chances for someone
To prove to us they are worthy of our love

Flower

If you love a flower
Don't pick it up
Let it grow
If you love a person
Don't own them
Let them explore

Ivy Rose Elizalde

You Complete You

You don't need anyone to complete you
You need to work on yourself
And be whole by yourself
Then find someone whom you can share
That fullness and abundance
You have so much in you

Choose

Choose someone who brings out the best in you
While accepting you for who you are
Not someone who pushes you through
Without understanding your flaws

Ivy Rose Elizalde

Rarer

It is rare to find someone
Who'll do everything for you
But it's rarer to find someone
Who won't let you.

Her Eyes Tell a Story

Eyes Speak

Your eyes speak more than words can say
As if they're asking for compassion
Of the pain and sorrow you try to hide
Which can't be seen but I feel how you tremble
Your eyes speak a lot of mystery inside

Ivy Rose Elizalde

Beam

Don't fall in love with her smile
Fall in love with her courage to beam
While wiping her tears
When nobody's looking

Change Me

I don't need a person who'll change me
I need someone who sees my flaws
But accepts me for who I am
Perhaps that will make me realize
He deserves the best
So I hope to change

Ivy Rose Elizalde

Wrong People

We meet the wrong people for reasons
To understand what we really want
And to realize what we truly deserve

Independent Woman

Heart needs to be broken
To understand emotions better
To step out of our comfort zones
And to become a lot stronger
Someone who lives on this earth
Who doesn't know how it feels
Will wonder all her life
The magic it has created
To an independent woman

Ivy Rose Elizalde

Mystery Behind Love

Sometimes we meet the wrong people
To remind us that love is a mystery
We'll never know who's right for us
Until we meet the right person

What is Enough?

Sometimes love isn't enough
What's enough is when two people decided
To respect and be faithful to each other
For the rest of their lives

Ivy Rose Elizalde

What is Love?

Love is when the other person's emotion
Becomes our own
It isn't just a feeling at all.

Not Everyday

It's not every day you meet someone
Who accepts your flaws
And adores your imperfection

Ivy Rose Elizalde

Right Name

Here I am again
Wishing for the stars
To whisper the right name
In case they find me
Miswriting it again

Fight For Me

If you want to make it work
Don't fight with me
Fight for me

Ivy Rose Elizalde

Love is Not Blind

Love is not blind for it can see thoroughly
But it can be complicated and unreasonable.

Onion

I can't help but smile at the thought
That onion can make me cry
More than love.

Ivy Rose Elizalde

Sincere Love

She just hope someone
Could remember her
Not by her face or name
But her truth
That she's the kind of person
Who asks for nothing
But sincere love

Her Eyes Tell a Story

Late

I guess you're a little late
To fix the mess that you've made
I already found the one
Who put my alphabet in order

Ivy Rose Elizalde

Confusion of Whom to Love

No matter how many times
We've been hurt in love
There's always another chance
To fall in love again
Sometimes it might take a while
But when fate plays with us
It could give us choices
And confusion of whom to love

The End

Our love may be a beautiful story
But it's not a fairytale
Our story has an ending
That for me is a happy one
We smiled and forgave each other
Then we move on with our own lives
Isn't that a wonderful ending?

Ivy Rose Elizalde

Preserve

When we preserve something
We patiently wait until it's ready
To make it lasts
Just like in love
We should wait for the right time
Until the love is ready
Because when love is preserved
Nothing and no one could destroy it.

Ivy Rose Elizalde

A Man Who Can Change

You can't ask a man to change
But a man who truly loves you
Will change himself
Without you even asking for it.

Vice Versa

Buy me a chocolate that could taste sweet
Though it's made of bitter additives
Buy me a flower that could stay fresh
Though it's slowly losing its leaves
Buy me a love that never fades
In a world of vice versa.

Ivy Rose Elizalde

Lost Boat

What if I didn't meet you?
Just like a lost boat
I might still be wandering around
Searching for my destination

Her Eyes Tell a Story

Home

I was lost in a place
That was familiar but empty
Then you came filling the pieces
Letting me find my way back home

Ivy Rose Elizalde

A Woman of Value

Isn't it fair for a woman to be treated well
For not asking for anything but love?
You can find a lot of gorgeous women in this world
But it's rare to find a woman of value

No Temporary

I haven't told you
I'm sick of temporary people
Temporary situation
Temporary feelings
I want someone
Who'll stay with me
Permanently

Ivy Rose Elizalde

Irony of Love

The more pain we experience in love
The more love we can offer
To the next one.

Chase the Light

In the midst of pain
You can see the light
That can lead you
To the direction of happiness
You just have to chase the light
And let go of the dark.

Decision

Love is more than just a feeling
It is more of a decision
We have to make for ourselves
To make things work out
Because in love
We are the ones who choose our happy ending

Ivy Rose Elizalde

Till it Happens

He makes you feel that you're the one
But he won't say anything
Like the stars would promise to fall one day
And you wait till it happens

I'm Enough

I'm not looking for love
In fact I let go of love in the past
What I'm looking for is compassion
Someone who would make me feel
That I'm enough
And would never let me go

Ivy Rose Elizalde

Love Competition

I can't fall in love with someone
Who gives a portion of his heart
I want it whole
I hate love competition

Uncertainty

When love is not a priority
But it's more than just a friendship
It's the uncertainty of connection
That often hurts us the most.

Ivy Rose Elizalde

Pure Love

I want you to remember her
And every time you'll hear her name
You'll regret losing her
Because she's a woman of pure love.

I See You

I can see a deep pain in your eyes
And wonder who's the reason behind
Because no matter how hard you try
To hide it within your smile
I see you like no one else
Your eyes will never lie.

Ivy Rose Elizalde

Security

The sense of security over someone
Isn't just being safe in their arms
But knowing they can accept you for who you are
And no one could steal them away from you

Sunset

Sunset made me realize
That some endings
Can be amazingly beautiful.

Ivy Rose Elizalde

Language of Souls

The way you speak to her
Is like you're talking to her soul
As if you know her pain
More than she thought she'll ever know
You understand her deep
Though she can't speak up her mind
It's the language of your souls
Learned through mastery of love

Stay Still

We may go where the wind blows
Or listen where our heart beats
But when we stay still and just feel
We'll see how the love is for real

Ivy Rose Elizalde

Accident

Love is an accident
We don't expect for its coming
Yet we hope for it.

Ride

When we drive without a destination
It's just enjoying the ride
While when we love without commitment
It's just enjoying the love
Without destination.

Ivy Rose Elizalde

One-Sided Love

I don't see a logic
In loving someone
Who can't love you back
Would you call it love
If it's one-sided?

Forgotten Dream

You visited me in my dream
The feelings were so real
Then I woke up and forgot the dream
But still remember how it feels.

Ivy Rose Elizalde

Falling

Falling in love is something
That comes at our unexpected
That's why it's called falling
'Cause no one knows when to fall.

Priority

Don't waste your time on someone
Who can't make you as a priority
Because if their love is true
You don't even have to ask for it.

Ivy Rose Elizalde

What She Wants

She doesn't want expensive gifts
Nor luxury cars won't impress her
She just wants your time and loyalty
And your real love is everything to her.

Who Won't Cheat

They often asked me
What I'm looking for in a guy
I guess our standard changes over time
Now I figured out what should be on top
A guy who won't cheat
That's number one important.

Ivy Rose Elizalde

Reason

We meet people for a reason
Doesn't matter what it is
Good or bad, we don't despise experience
We learn from them
That's how life becomes life.

Star

We never know the value of a star
'Cause their brilliance and presence
Serves no purpose to us
Perhaps if they never show up again
We start missing them.

Ivy Rose Elizalde

Enough

Let me love you in a way
You won't worry
If the sun won't shine
Because I give you enough light.

Feel

If you're unsure if a person loves you
Then maybe he's wondering too
Because a person who truly loves you
Will make it sure he makes you feel
Exactly the way he feels for you

Ivy Rose Elizalde

Never Test

Never test the water
Unless you don't trust its purity.

Beautiful Dream

I started to see you as a perfect guy
In a beautiful dream
But it worries me a lot
Because that perfect guy never exists
I wish you're not just a part
Of this beautiful dream.

Ivy Rose Elizalde

Amazing

How love can make you say
A thousand words
Without saying a word
Is simply amazing.

Imagine

Imagine how our life could have been
If our paths have never crossed
Could we possibly believe
In a love that lasts forever?

Ivy Rose Elizalde

A Game of Love

Often love plays game
A game of testing one's feelings
To make sure if it's genuine
A game of not saying a word
For someone to keep on guessing
I'm so tired of those games
If you want to make this work
Just be direct with your feelings

Stolen

We knew this love was not for us
Yet we're little stubborn and took a chance
Wishing on a time we have stolen
To change its plan about us.

Ivy Rose Elizalde

I Won't Settle

I won't settle for someone
Who treat me as an option
I won't settle for someone
Who's uncertain of me
I want someone who'll stare at me
With overflowing certainty of love
in his eyes.

"My heart found its home, the moment I found you."

Found

I Found You

I look at you and just couldn't believe
How am I supposed to find you
In this world where love is just a word
Till you came, bringing that word into life

Ivy Rose Elizalde

My Heart Belongs to You

I'll give you time to figure out
If your love for me is true
Though it might bring tears to me
If you found somebody new
But if you'll still choose me
In spite of everything that we've been through
Then maybe I could say
That my heart belongs to you.

Stay

I'm no longer into that whirlwind kind of emotion
I just want someone who's sincere
Who'll give to me his heart and won't take it back
I want someone who will stay

Ivy Rose Elizalde

Inseparable

Let's go to a place
Where letting go is forbidden
Where saying goodbye is a bad word
Where telling a lie is not practice
Where you and I are inseparable

Calm

You made me realize
That love shouldn't be hard
It's like the calmness of the night
That made us sound asleep
The silence of the waves
That gave us peace of mind

Ivy Rose Elizade

Mornings

They say you're in love
When mornings won't make you feel tired anymore

Surprisingly

How would you know you finally found the one?
Surprisingly, when you meet the person
You'll just know.

Ivy Rose Elizalde

Oxygen

I'm not yet into you
All I know is that you're an oxygen
I can't afford to lose now

Definition of Love

As we get older the definition of love changes
It's no longer a challenge or a chasing game
It's simply pure intentions
That could give us peace of mind

Ivy Rose Elizalde

A Sweet Escape

A simple touch of your hand
Gives comfort to my soul
A sweet escape from the pain
That's slowly killing me.

New Meaning of Love

I thought I knew everything about love
Until I met you
You gave a new meaning to it

Ivy Rose Elizalde

Pain

The moment I realize
I've fallen in love with you
Is the moment I felt your pain
'Cause I'm hurting too.

First Met

I remember how we first met
And I realize that love can hide
Into disgusting firsts

Ivy Rose Elizalde

Coffee

I don't want flowers
Just bring me a coffee
I would love you for that

Lost with Your Smile

I asked for a direction
You said just straight ahead
You said it with a smile
And so I'm lost again

Ivy Rose Elizalde

Rainbow

You make it easy for me to smile
Just how the rainbows were made
To make the sky forgets its sadness

Longing

I wait for the winter to come
To touch the first snow on my palm
How wonderful it brings
To feel the love through the coldness
Just like the joy of a longing heart

Ivy Rose Elizalde

Rare Gem

Once in our life we had a precious diamond
Yet we ignore its value
Until it's gone
Still we found a lot of stones
But they're just good for nothing
Up till life gives us another chance
To see a rare gem
And we know once we let it go
We won't find another kind
Because a rare gem can only be found
Once or twice in our lifetime

Call my Name

You never know how my heart skips a beat
Each time you call my name
Such a sweet voice touching my soul
Letting me hold its softness

Ivy Rose Elizalde

Forgive Me

Forgive me if I make you doubt
The extent of love I have for you
Perhaps I've got issues on my past
To master not to fully give my heart.

The Best Kind of Love

The best kind of love
Is when you can be selfless at times
But know how to stir it with self-love

Ivy Rose Elizalde

Apart

If missing someone means their absence
Why do I feel your presence but still miss you?
Like an air I cannot touch but feel
Like the longing of your love
I sense growing every day
A consequence of being apart
It's like you're dragging away my heart

The Existence of True Love

I cried a lot because of love
Shedding tears like rain that just won't stop
It's because I believed
In an illusion of true love
At this time I'm sobbing again
But with joys right before my eyes
As you gave me reasons to believe again
In the existence of true love

Ivy Rose Elizalde

Voice

Your voice is like the sound of the waves
That brings calmness in my heart
Leaving gentle whisper in my ear
Dancing in the silence of the ocean

Stare

At times I stare at you
Like my eyes have seen a sea of stars
Perhaps I'm wondering
How my heart finds it's way to you.

Ivy Rose Elizalde

The Way to Her Heart

The way to her heart
Is not through her stomach
Not even through her stubborn mind
Rather through the deepness of her soul
That if you can reach
Then she's yours.

Let's Take a Walk

Let's take a walk
To understand each other more
To talk about each other's lives
And have a wonderful connection
We don't have to run
Let's take it slow
Let's take a walk
It's a journey of our love

Ivy Rose Elizalde

Reminisce

Let's go back to the place where we first met
To remind us how funny it was
That little awkwardness we had
Turned out to be the moments we'll gonna share
For the rest of our lives

Forever Can Exists

I asked you until when
Those eyes will stare at me
Like they want me to believe
In the existence of forever
Then you smiled and said
"Till forever can exists"

Ivy Rose Elizalde

Today

Let's not overthink about the past
Nor worry about the future
Rather we focus on today
And repeat that every day

Choosing You

The surest thing I've ever done
Was choosing you.

Ivy Rose Elizalde

Patience

Will I ever find someone
Whose heart knows no boundaries
In letting off my flaws
Who understands all my miseries
Who pardons my mistakes
And won't leave me at stake
A man who's a master of patience
That's all I see in you

Meant

No matter how long it takes
Always believe that there is someone out there
Who's meant just for you
And you'll meet when you're both ready
To understand that loving
And receiving love in return
Is the key to everlasting love

Ivy Rose Elizalde

Catch

Someone throws my heart
And I see you catching on air
Wishing it lands on your direction

Tease

A guy who adores you
Will tease you to make you laugh
Not the one to be laughed about

Ivy Rose Elizalde

Fix Our Fate

Let's travel to the future
To see if we're destined together
And if we're not
Let's fix our fate
And try even harder

Her Eyes Tell a Story

Candid

There are times you might see me upset
That I can no longer hold back the tears
You're the only one who can see my pain
As if you sense how I really feel
I don't know how you do it
But you made it easy for me
To be something candid

Ivy Rose Elizalde

Compassion

How could I forget such sweetness?
I live a hundred years to realize
A man with compassion
Was never easy to find

Comfort Zone

You don't realize
How you brighten up my day
And calm my helpless night
You are my home
My comfort zone

Ivy Rose Elizalde

Difference

We meet a lot of wrong people
To make us realize
The difference of being with the right person.

Her Eyes Tell a Story

Best Feeling

The best feeling in this world
Is when somebody tells you
You're the best thing
That ever happened to him
And you believe in him.

Ivy Rose Elizalde

Loved

She's more than grateful to understand
The real meaning of being loved
It's how you adore and respect her
And remain faithful in her absence

Give

I will give you my hand
To protect your heart from sorrows
I will give you my heart
To protect your hand from mistakes.

Ivy Rose Elizalde

No Promises

You didn't promise
You won't leave me
But I know you won't.

Are You In Love?

They say you're in love
When somebody compliments about your shirt
And then you wear it every day.

Ivy Rose Elizalde

Staring into My Soul

The way you look at me
Is like you're staring into my soul
As if you're telling me
We've already met before.

Touch

The touch of your hand
Gives comfort to my soul
Like a home
I finally come to rest.

Ivy Rose Elizalde

Write Our Destiny

We are running out of time
I have to tell you how I feel
Before the sun goes down
And the star shines into the sky
Let's write our destiny.

Linger

Maybe we met at the wrong time
Somehow we knew it could be so hard
But even though waiting's a boring game
I'll still linger on till the day is right for us.

Ivy Rose Elizalde

Special

He just want to make her feel special
But the woman started to see
A different guy in him
He's special, a one of a kind.

Don't Break My Rule

Tell me you won't make promises
Let's work it out without a word
But please don't break my rule
"Don't ever let me go".

Ivy Rose Elizalde

That One Person

I grasped peace on my own
But I never knew that love could bring
A novel meaning of peace
It's like waking up in the morning
Knowing you can get through anything
With that one person
Who believes in you.

Addicted with Your Love

You filled my life with happiness
And you never get tired of listening
To my never-ending stories
I can't imagine a life without you
I'm already addicted with your love

Ivy Rose Elizalde

I Was

I became a self-reliant woman
Never needed a man in my life
I'd been happy on my own
I thought I was, until I met you.

Crazy in Love

I won't leave you
Even the world would disagree
I still believe in you
Even if you say stars aren't beautiful.

Ivy Rose Elizalde

Why Not?

He asked me why I love him
I can't think of an answer
So I asked him back
"Why not?"

Knowing you is the best thing that ever happened to me
Everything I dreamt about
Visited my reality
I've waited for someone who'll love me for my scars
Now you're holding my heart
Making the stars dance in the moonlight
On our skies who won't promise anything
Rather show its magic
An ocean of love can bring
Leaving the world wonders
Escaping the universe
Staying with your love is all I need

About the Author

Ivy Rose Elizalde started to write poems about love when she was only 13 years old, inspired by her teenage crush. Since then, she realized she could write and it became her hobby. She began to write poems not only about love but also about everything in life.

As years passed, she had her heart broken, and suddenly lost interest in writing. For a long period of time, she stopped writing.

As she matures, she became interested in reading finance books. Eventually she got inspired to write a book on her own about financial literacy with a goal to share in a book all the things that have change her life.

While she was thinking of the next book she will going to write, she's thinking of a book that will inspire her to write every single day, then she remembered her first love which is poetry. Then she tried to write again, and she writes with her heart.

She's a Filipina, registered nurse, with the passion to touch souls through writing.

Lightning Source UK Ltd.
Milton Keynes UK
UKHW021015210820
368606UK00012B/1042